# The Story of the Suffragettes

Written by Joanna N

T0364501

## Contents

**Collins**

# Who were the suffragettes?

In the UK today, almost every adult has the right to vote. That means that, as soon as you turn 18, whether you're a boy or a girl, you'll be able to have your say at a general election in how the country is being run. So if you don't like a law, you can vote for a **Member of Parliament (MP)** who is more likely to change that law. You can even stand as an MP yourself, and really make a difference.

a housewife in the 1890s

the Houses of Parliament in London, UK

2

But fewer than a hundred years ago, our country was a very different place. Only wealthy men were allowed to make the laws, or vote to change the laws. Few women went to school, and the ones who did rarely made use of their education. Instead, they were expected to stay at home, looking after

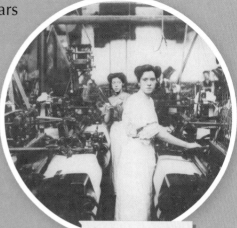

factory workers in the 1890s

their husband and children. The women who did go out to work were restricted to jobs like factory work, domestic service, nursing and teaching, but these were not well paid, and the work in factories was also exhausting and dangerous. That's the world the suffragettes were born into, and the world they vowed to change.

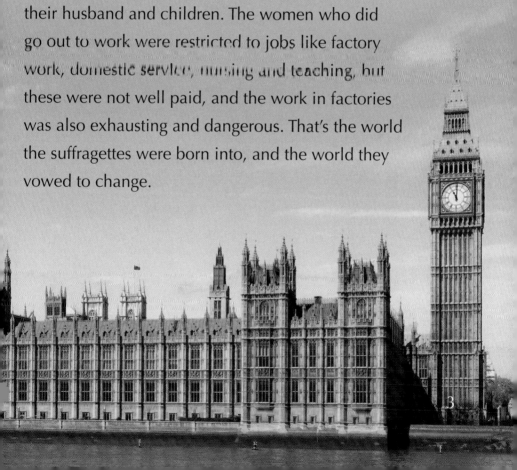

The suffragettes were a group of women who came together in the late 19th century and early 20th century to fight for women's "suffrage", which means "right to vote". They believed that women should be equal in the eyes of the law, and so should get the same rights as men did to choose their MP. This wasn't a battle purely for the sake of equality though; the suffragettes wanted to be able to vote so they could make a difference to the lives of working women.

suffragettes protesting in London in 1912 to win women the right to vote

a policeman trying to remove a suffragette from the railings outside Buckingham Palace in 1914

Over the course of nearly a hundred years, the numbers of women joining the movement grew and grew. Together, they campaigned by peacefully making their case to **Parliament** and, later, by more aggressive demonstrations to grab attention, from chaining themselves to railings to setting fire to postboxes. The story of the suffragettes is one of struggle, sacrifice and endless setbacks. But it is, ultimately, a victorious one. We have these thousands of women to thank for the more equal world we live in today. This is their story.

# Voting in the early 19th century

Today, we believe that being allowed to vote is one of our most basic rights. But in the early 19th century, voting wasn't seen as a right for all, but as a **privilege** for the well-off "upper" classes. As such, you could only vote if you were male, over the age of 21 and owned a large property.

This meant that women, as well as many middle-class and working-class men – for example, those who worked on the land or in shops or factories – had no say in the running of the country.

In 1832, Parliament changed the law to give the vote to tenant farmers (those who rented their land), shopkeepers, and anyone who paid rent of ten pounds or more a year. Women, however, remained excluded, and not just from voting.

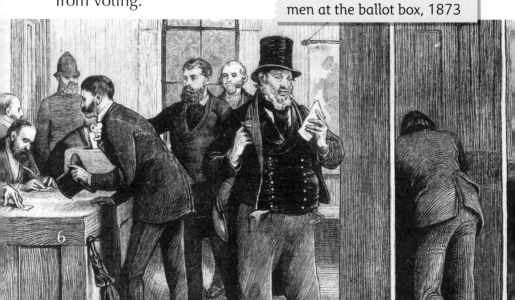

men at the ballot box, 1873

# Women in the workplace

While most working-class women had to work in order to support their families, this was largely confined to domestic service, which meant cooking and cleaning for wealthy households, or working in factories where the hours were long and the work hard and often dangerous. Even if they did want to work, upper-class and middle-class women were still limited to roles such as governesses, music teachers, or nurses. Jobs like vet, lawyer and doctor were strictly seen as men-only. Women were, however, allowed to own property and had to give part of their income, called "tax", to the government, just like men.

domestic service in the 1890s

# The early fight for equality

For the large part of the early 1800s, the Conservative or Tory party was in charge of the country, and opposed all changes to Parliament and voting. But in 1830, the Tory Prime Minister was replaced by the Liberal or "Whig" Earl Grey. He passed the 1832 **Reform Act**, which gave more men the right to vote.

But if women were allowed to own houses like men, and had to pay tax like men, then surely they should be allowed to have a say in how the country was run, like men? That was the argument that women and some men began to voice in the early 1800s.

Earl Grey

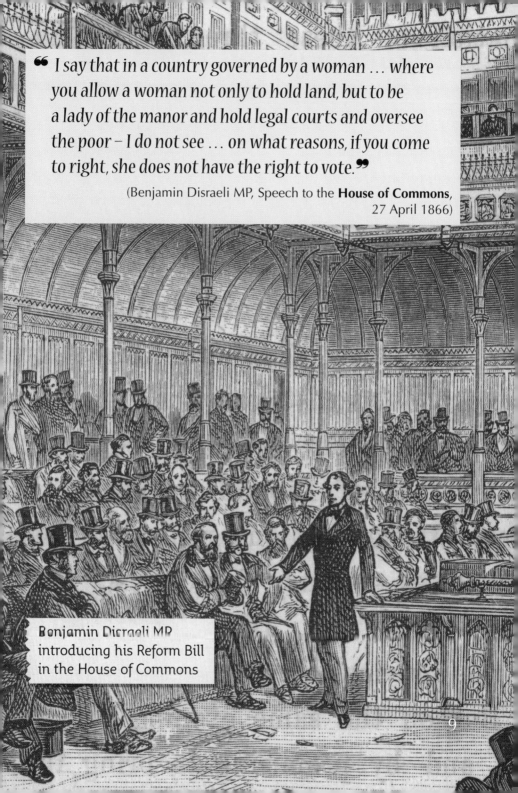

66 I say that in a country governed by a woman … where you allow a woman not only to hold land, but to be a lady of the manor and hold legal courts and oversee the poor – I do not see … on what reasons, if you come to right, she does not have the right to vote. 99

(Benjamin Disraeli MP, Speech to the **House of Commons**, 27 April 1866)

Benjamin Disraeli MP introducing his Reform Bill in the House of Commons

9

# Anti-suffragists

In 1832, Mary Smith presented the first ever women's suffrage petition to Parliament, demanding the right to vote. However, the demand was ignored, and would continue to be so for decades to come. **Opposition** to women's suffrage was loud and widespread. Most men and many women of all

Queen Victoria

classes believed the idea to be ridiculous. Queen Victoria herself called it a "mad, wicked **folly**".

The anti-suffragists argued that women didn't need to vote, because their fathers, husbands or brothers could, and that was enough. Some insisted that most women were just not clever enough to understand politics. There was also concern that if women got ideas above their station, then they would abandon family life and society would fall apart. And, despite the Women's Suffrage Society collecting 1,500 signatures on a petition that they presented to Parliament in 1866, many MPs claimed most women didn't even want the vote and wouldn't use it if they got it.

Parliament did agree to listen to the women's arguments, though. So every year a group of women would go to Westminster to make their case. And every year, the male MPs would ignore them, knowing that, as women couldn't vote, they couldn't vote them out of a job. Besides, as they saw it, there weren't enough of them demanding the vote. But things were about to change.

## Changing times

The Isle of Man gave women who owned property the right to vote in 1881.

anti-suffrage cartoon from 1910

# The Kensington Society

❝ None but intellectual women are admitted and therefore it is not likely to become a merely **puerile** and gossiping Society. ❞

(Letter from Alice Westlake to Helen Taylor)

Initially formed in 1865 as a women's discussion group, one of the topics up for debate at the Kensington Society that year was women's suffrage. The group voted overwhelmingly in favour of women's suffrage, and drafted a petition to demand that Parliament give women the right to vote. Alongside the Manchester Committee for the **Enfranchisement** of Women, whose membership included Richard Pankhurst, they took their petition to two sympathetic Liberal MPs – John Stuart Mill and Henry Fawcett – who drafted a change or "amendment" to the Reform Act.

John Stuart Mill

Henry Fawcett

The amendment was defeated, but the women of the Kensington Society were determined to fight on, renaming themselves the London Society for Women's Suffrage. Henry Fawcett's wife, Millicent, joined, and quickly became leader of the London suffragists. By the end of the 19th century, she had expanded her horizons still further.

## MILLICENT GARRETT FAWCETT (1847–1929)

Millicent set up and led the National Union of Women's Suffrage Societies (NUWSS), the largest suffrage organisation, which campaigned peacefully for votes for women. She also helped found the women-only Newnham College, part of Cambridge University. Her sister, Elizabeth Garrett Anderson, became the country's first female doctor.

# The National Union of Women's Suffrage Societies (NUWSS)

In 1884, the Third Reform Act gave many working-class men the right to vote for the first time. Outraged that these men, many of whom could barely read or write, were to be allowed to vote while they weren't, more and more educated, middle-class women began to join or form new local suffrage societies as a way of coming together to make their voices heard.

When Millicent set up the NUWSS in 1897, she brought more than 20 suffrage societies from London to Edinburgh under the same banner. By giving these separate groups one clear voice and set of aims, she believed they'd stand a better chance of getting what they wanted. Together, they aimed to change hearts and minds by civilised argument and peaceful demonstrations alone. And they made some strides, persuading politicians to back their cause, and getting **bills** before Parliament.

But in Manchester, one family was beginning to get frustrated with the lack of progress made by the NUWSS, and vowed to take matters into its own hands. Its decision was to change the course of the campaign, and history itself.

Millicent Fawcett addressing a meeting in Hyde Park, 1913

HAIRMAN
M ROBERTSON
PEAKER
FAWCETT

10

NATIONAL UNION of WOMEN'S SUFFRAGE SOC ES
PRESIDENT M RS FAWCET
LAW-ABIDING SUFFRAGI

# "Deeds not words"

> 66 We women suffragists have a great mission –
> the greatest mission the world has ever known.
> It is to free half the human race, and through
> that freedom save the rest. 99
>
> (Emmeline Pankhurst, speech at the Albert Hall in London
> 17 October 1912)

Emmeline Pankhurst was the wife of Richard Pankhurst, a well-known political **activist**, and had fought to improve the lives of working-class people for many years. Following her husband's death, she was forced to take a job working amongst the poor in Manchester. Seeing for herself the terrible conditions many women

Emmeline Pankhurst

had to endure, she realised the need for change was urgent, and knew the only way to get that change was by getting women the right to vote. That way, they could argue for new laws that would improve their lives.

So in 1903, along with two of her daughters, Christabel and Sylvia, Emmeline formed a new suffrage society, called the Women's Social and Political Union (WSPU). In contrast to the peaceful campaigning of the NUWSS, whose slogan was "law-abiding suffragists", the WSPU took the fight to the streets, under Emmeline's motto: "deeds not words".

women advertising the WSPU from a boat on the Thames

17

# Early action

The first of the WSPU's "deeds" was to publicly pester politicians, in a bid to embarrass the men, and bring attention to its cause. In October 1905, Christabel Pankhurst and Annie Kenney went to a Liberal party rally in Manchester and heckled Sir Edward Grey on voting rights. They were arrested for assault and obstruction, and became the first suffragettes to be put in prison, a landmark in itself. This raised awareness of the WSPU amongst the press and public, and marked a turning point, as more women were made aware not just of the unfairness of their situation, but of the possibility of change as well.

Annie Kenney is arrested during a demonstration.

# Christabel Pankhurst
## (1880–1958)

The eldest daughter of Emmeline, Christabel studied Law at university, but because she was a woman wasn't allowed to actually be a lawyer. One of the founders of the WSPU, she was also one of the first suffragettes to be arrested. Many more women joined the movement after her trial.

# Rallies and marches

The Pankhursts' hopes of victory had grown when the Liberal party took over government in 1905, as in the past the Liberals had been far more supportive of women's suffrage than the Conservatives. But the Prime Minister Henry Campbell-Bannerman, and his **Chancellor**, Henry Herbert Asquith, refused to even meet the women. With the newspapers ignoring the women as well, the Pankhursts needed a new tactic, and more voices to help them make their case.

Until then, the fight for women's suffrage had largely been a middle-class one. But Sylvia planned to persuade poorer women from the East End of London to join – those who worked in laundries and factories. Emmeline wasn't convinced it would work, but in February 1906 Sylvia led 300 women from the East End to join a thousand-strong march to Westminster. Newspapers could no longer ignore the women, and the Daily Mail dubbed the campaigners "suffragettes", a term many found insulting, but which stuck, nonetheless.

# Sylvia Pankhurst (1882–1960)

The second daughter of Emmeline, Sylvia, was a talented artist and went to art school in London, but devoted her life to politics. She ran the East End headquarters of the WSPU and was behind some of the suffragettes' most daring and destructive campaigns, including arson. She was frequently arrested and force-fed.

Men and women from the women's suffrage movement march through London.

The Pankhursts organised more **rallies**, with the number of suffragettes growing every time. One rally attracted 7,000 supporters. Faced with such numbers, the Prime Minister finally agreed to speak to a small group. Around 300 women went to Westminster to meet him, where he said he was sympathetic to their cause, but could do nothing about it because neither his **cabinet** nor the country was ready for such change. The suffragettes, though, were determined to make them ready, by any means necessary.

Suffragettes parade through London.

# Breaking the law

Every year, Parliament has an official opening, marked by a speech from the king or queen. It's an important day, as the monarch tells the country what laws the government will look at in the coming 12 months.

So in 1907, Emmeline Pankhurst chose that day to lead 400 women in a march to Parliament. They were blocked at Westminster Abbey by **battalions** of police who began riding horses into the crowd to scatter them, or shoving them into side alleys. The battle lasted for hours and ended with 54 women being arrested, including Sylvia and Christabel Pankhurst.

When newspapers printed the story, the public was shocked and the suffragettes gained support. But another attempt to change the law on voting was rejected. Angered by this, and knowing that it would bring them maximum newspaper coverage, the suffragettes started to deliberately break the law.

Emmeline Pankhurst speaking at Trafalgar Square.

They began attacking MPs with flour, tomatoes and stink bombs, and slapping and spitting at police. When Henry Asquith, who was Prime Minister by then, ignored a rally of a quarter of a million suffragettes in Hyde Park, women broke the windows of his home in Downing Street and chained themselves to the railings to get his attention.

After being arrested, these women chose to go to prison rather than pay a fine. By becoming **martyrs**, they reasoned they would get more newspaper coverage, and more support and sympathy, as the public knew that to choose prison was a desperate measure indeed.

Women chain themselves to railings at 10 Downing Street.

# What about the men?

While most men were against the idea of women voting, it would be wrong to assume all of them were. A few Liberal MPs spoke up for the suffragettes in Parliament, whilst many other men attended rallies and marches. A few men even fought alongside them, getting arrested and imprisoned as well.

A man signs the NUWS petition for votes for women.

## HERBERT HENRY ASQUITH (1852–1928)

Asquith trained as a lawyer, but went into politics in 1886 as a Liberal MP, eventually becoming Prime Minister from 1908 to 1916. Known as the "sledgehammer" because of his ability to argue, he fought against women's suffrage throughout his career, only eventually coming round to the idea towards the end of the First World War.

# Standing together

In 1908, the WSPU adopted the colours purple, green and white for their banners, flags and sashes, as well as wearing white dresses. It helped unite them, and mark them out, so that the opposition could recognise a suffragette, and see just how many of them there were.

Dedicated to THE WOMEN'S SOCIAL AND POLITICAL UNION.

**THE MARCH OF THE WOMEN**
( Popular Edition in F..To be sung in Unison )
By **ETHEL SMYTH**, Mus.Doc.
Price: One Shilling & Sixpence net.

> **"** Purple as everyone knows is the royal colour. It stands for the royal blood that flows in the veins of every suffragette, the instinct of freedom and dignity ... white stands for purity in private and public life ... green is the colour of hope and the emblem of spring. **"**
>
> (Emmeline Pethick-Lawrence, editor of the weekly newspaper, *Votes for Women*)

# Prison and punishment

Between 1905 and 1914, around 1,000 suffragettes were sent to prison. It can't have been an easy option for any of them as prison in the early 20th century was bleak. The conditions in the cells were appalling, with only planks of wood for a bed, a thin mattress, and a bucket for water and for going to the toilet at night. Food was thin porridge or gruel for every meal, and inmates were only allowed outside to exercise twice a week. The government hoped this would make the suffragettes give up their fight, but it just made them even more determined to win. And they had a brutal tactic of their own: in 1909, they started to go on hunger strike.

Suffragettes wave through the bars from their cells in Holloway Prison.

# Hunger strikes

Believing that the government would have no choice
but to release them if they were starving, many
suffragettes refused to eat any food at all. This was
a dangerous decision. Although the body can go for weeks
without food, it becomes weak and internal organs can
become damaged. Knowing this, the government ordered
warders to tempt the women with delicious food, like roast
chicken, instead of gruel, believing they would give in.
But the women stayed true to their cause and turned
it down. The government's next move was a shocking one.
It ordered warders to forcibly feed the women by pouring
milk into tubes that had been fed into their stomachs.

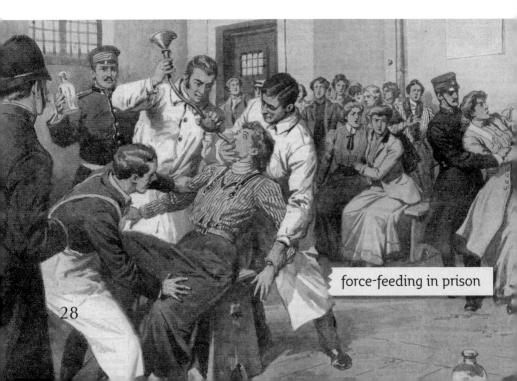

force-feeding in prison

> 66 You feel quite stunned and dizzy and do a great deal of spitting for some time after the tube is withdrawn. You also have an ache in your chest and feel very sick. 99
>
> (From a letter to Miss Wallace Dunlop from Laura Ainsworth, 1909)

Force-feeding is painful and dangerous, and the decision to use it angered the public and many politicians. But Asquith didn't care, and many more women had to suffer the agony on a regular basis, including Sylvia Pankhurst and Emily Davison.

## EMILY WILDING DAVISON (1872–1913)

Emily Davison undertook some of the suffragettes' most daring attacks, including setting fire to a postbox. She also hid in a cupboard in Parliament on census night in 1911, so that she could claim to live in the House of Commons and so demand the same political rights as the men who were MPs there. She was arrested nine times, and force-fed 49 times.

# Sacrifices for the cause

Going to prison wasn't just a hardship in terms of putting up with poor conditions and force-feeding. The women were also risking their status in society, and some, their families' livelihoods.

For the wealthier suffragettes, a criminal record brought shame to their families, as prison was largely seen as a punishment for poor people.

suffragettes in prison clothing after their release

NATIONAL WOMEN'S
SOCIAL
AND

For working-class women, the sacrifice was far greater. As well as relying on the women to look after the children, families often depended on their income for survival. But if the women were in prison, they weren't working,

a woman and child begging

which meant they weren't earning, which meant they couldn't put food on the table. Even when they were released, they might find themselves out of a job, as factory owners deemed them unreliable or troublemakers.

## LADY CONSTANCE LYTTON (1869–1923)

Lady Constance Lytton used her status as an aristocrat to lobby Parliament along with her brother, but she also joined the WSPU under the alias "Jane", so that if she were arrested she wouldn't get preferential treatment because of her position. In prison, she went on hunger strike and was force-fed.

# A campaign of destruction

Outside prison, the war between suffragettes and politicians raged on. In 1910, hopes were raised as another suffrage bill, called the **Conciliation** Bill, came before Parliament. This bill, which would give property-owning women over the age of 30 the right to vote, was actually passed by Parliament at a second reading. But a bill needs three readings to become law, and Asquith, who still opposed suffrage, quickly decided to "dissolve" Parliament and call a general election, saying there wasn't time for a third reading before the election. Understandably, the suffragettes were outraged.

THE RIGHT DISHONOURABLE DOUBLE-FACE ASQUITH.

A.PATRIOT.

*Citizen Asq—th:* "Down with privilege of birth —up with democratic rule!"

*Monseigneur Asq—th:* "The rights of Government belong to the aristocrats by birth—men. No liberty or equality for woman!"

**VOTES FOR WOMEN.**

Women! The Government refuse to give you the vote. Therefore, work against the Liberal Candidate, the nominee of the Government.

Electors! The Government pose as champions of the Constitution, but deny constitutional liberty to women. We call upon you to support the Women.

Vote against the Government and keep the Liberal out.

In response, on 18th November, the WSPU sent a group of 300 women to Parliament to protest. As they tried to force their way into the House of Commons, they were met by police who assaulted the women, beating them with helmets, and throwing them on to the ground and even into the crowds of men gathered to watch, some of whom attacked them too. Emmeline begged the police to arrest the women but, knowing that prison sentences made the public more sympathetic towards the women, the police instead vowed to tire them out. However, after four hours of battle, the police gave in and arrested a total of 119 women and men.

The day became known as Black Friday, the most brutal of the campaign so far. Those arrested, however, were never charged because the new Home Secretary, Winston Churchill, was determined to keep details of police violence out of the courts, a fact that surely enraged Emmeline even further.

a suffragette struggling with a policeman on "Black Friday"

# Broken windows

In 1912, the suffragettes began a mass window smashing
campaign, targeting not just government offices but also
shops, men's clubs and newspapers that were opposed to
their cause. Using stones and hammers, the women and
their male supporters caused hundreds of pounds' worth
of damage. They hoped insurance companies would get
so tired of paying for replacement panes of glass that they
would start to lobby the government and demand they
listen to the suffragettes.

suffragettes smashing
windows, 1912

34

> **"** In my right hand I had a hammer, my pockets of my raincoat were bulging with pebbles – bang went my hammer … And I walked down the Strand as though I was playing hockey, and I just boldly went on like that, and I did at least nine windows. **"**
>
> (Charlotte "Charlie" Marsh)

But broken windows were not the suffragettes' only weapon, or the most dangerous. Christabel Pankhurst also planned a secret campaign of arson, targeting the homes of government ministers.

The home of MP Arthur du Cros was burnt down by a suffagette arson attack, 1913.

Having successfully damaged a house being built for the current chancellor, Lloyd George, the suffragettes increased the number of arson attacks, setting fire to public buildings like railway stations, theatres, cricket pavilions and racecourse stands, and scorching slogans into the turf. In a bid to hit communications networks, they poured chemicals into postboxes, and cut telephone wires. Emily Davison even announced to newspapers what her plans were, in the hope of gaining more attention and getting arrested. She succeeded in doing that after setting fire to a postbox. The suffragettes were blazing a trail of destruction, and would stop at nothing, it seemed, to get their way.

Daisy Dugdale leading a procession

# The Cat and Mouse Act

Asquith was beginning to panic. Daily life was being affected by the attacks, and the public was being put at risk, meaning the people might turn on the government. On top of that, with more women than ever in prison and on hunger strike, there was the chance that one of them might die, gaining even more sympathy for the cause. So in 1913, in a bid to end the hunger strikes and weaken the suffragettes' resolve, Asquith introduced a new law.

This law would allow prisons to release the women who were ill from starvation and let them recover at home, and then lock them up once they were well again. It became known as the Cat and Mouse Act.

# The final push

Emily Wilding Davison was one of the most active and determined suffragettes and there was little she wouldn't do to help the cause. In prison, in a bid to end force-feeding, she tried to kill herself, believing that "one big tragedy might save many others". But after throwing herself twice over iron railings and once down a staircase, she only managed to injure herself and, as soon as she was conscious again, she was force-fed. The following year, though, saw her most daring act to date: an act that was also to be her last.

Emily Davison's attempt to stop the king's horse at the Epsom Derby

Derby Day at Epsom was the country's most famous horse race, attended by many important people. On 4th June 1913, King George V himself was attending as his own horse was running. Determined to get the king's attention, and knowing that newspapers around the world would cover the event, Emily vowed to wave a suffragette banner in front of him.

As the horses stampeded around Tattenham Corner, Emily slipped under the railing and seemed to throw herself into the approaching pack before the jockeys had time to pull up. She was trampled underfoot and died four days later of a fractured skull.

> ❝ It was all over so quickly. Emily was under the hooves of one of the horses and seemed to be hurled for some distance across the grass. The horse stumbled sideways and its jockey was thrown from its back. She lay very still. ❞
>
> (Mary Richardson)

Emily Davison's funeral procession

No one knows if Emily Davison intended to die that day – she set off from home with a return train ticket and a ticket to a suffragette dance that evening in her bag – and many believe she only intended to pin a banner on the king's horse. But her death secured the attention and public sympathy for the cause she had so craved. Her funeral was attended by thousands of women and tens of thousands more supporters lined the streets of London as her coffin passed by.

After the horrors of hunger strikes and the death of Emily Davison, public sympathy for suffragettes and support for their cause had increased. However, the First World War, declared in 1914, was also to play a crucial part in women's fight for the right to vote.

With so many men leaving home to join the army and navy, women were needed on the home front. The suffragettes were released from prison, and the WSPU suspended its campaign to focus on the more urgent fight at hand. Women began to play a bigger role in society, taking over jobs that would have been done by their husbands, brothers and fathers, as well as an essential one in the war itself.

Suffragette Mary Sophia Allen inspects her female police force in 1915.

41

# Women at war

Even at the turn of the 20th century, men were still regarded as the real income earners with less than a third of the workforce made up of women. On top of that, women were still very limited in what jobs they were allowed, or expected to do, with many employers refusing to take on married women, and most single women being servants or doing "piece work" at home, such as washing, sewing or ironing. But with so many men fighting overseas, the social rules had to be quickly forgotten, and women found themselves not only running their own homes, but also going outside it to earn wages for the first time as well.

While some women had worked as nurses before the war, and a tiny few as doctors, many more began medical training. More women trained as teachers, while others found work in shops and offices. **Munitions** factories took on hundreds of women too, paying them far more than they had earned at home doing piece work.

By 1918, there were a record five million working women in the UK, many experiencing a level of independence they had never before known, as well as far greater respect from men.

a munitions factory during the First World War

an ambulance driver maintaining her vehicle

It was this change that helped to convince many more MPs and ministers that women could do anything that men could, and so deserved the vote. With Asquith gone and a new Prime Minister, David Lloyd George, who supported women's suffrage in place, there was a better chance than ever of victory. On top of that, the law on voting was about to be changed anyway.

women war workers meeting David Lloyd George

A woman reads a copy of the *Suffragette* magazine on an open-top London bus.

A general election was due in 1918, and the government had realised that none of the millions of soldiers returning from the war would be allowed to vote because they hadn't owned or lived in property long enough. Worried the men might start a revolution, they decided a new law was needed as a matter of urgency, and this time, as well as abolishing the rules on property for men, there would be a clause – Clause IV – which would give women over the age of 30 the right to vote too.

> **"** To live to see the triumph of a 'lost' cause for which we have suffered so much and would have suffered everything, must be almost the greatest of delights. **"**
>
> (Evelyn Sharp)

# Votes for women

By the time the Representation of the People Bill (or Fourth Reform Bill) came to be voted on in Parliament in June 1917, the tide had turned in favour of the suffragettes. Only 55 MPs opposed Clause IV, compared to 385 in favour. Even the **House of Lords** had been won over, and the bill became law the following year.

The 50-year fight for the right to vote had cost many women their health, and in Emily Davison's case, her life, but it had finally been won. And by 1928, the law had been improved again to include all women over the age of 21, meaning they were on an equal footing with men for the first time. However, voting was just the beginning of the role women were to play in politics.

Women cast their votes for the first time in the 1918 General Election.

Just weeks ahead of the 1918 General Election, a bill was passed at the last minute that gave women the right to become MPs. Sixteen women, including Christabel Pankhurst, stood for Parliament. Only one was elected, and she chose not to take her seat but, the following year, Nancy Astor became the country's first female MP. Since then, the number of women in high-profile political roles has grown year on year.

Nancy Astor campaigning for votes

# From then to now

In 1924, Margaret Bondfield became the first female minister. She went on to become the first female **cabinet minister** too, in 1929. In 1975, a grocer's daughter called Margaret Thatcher became the leader of the Conservative party, and in 1979, became Britain's first female Prime Minister. And in 2014, Nicola Sturgeon became the First Minister for Scotland, the first woman to do so.

Margaret Bondfield at 10 Downing Street in London

Margaret Thatcher

Nicola Sturgeon

Women have helped make some important changes in the law as well. In the early 1920s, Eleanor Rathbone campaigned successfully for a universal family allowance that would help ease poverty. Importantly, it was to be paid directly to the mother, not the father. This is now known as Child Benefit, and is still usually paid to mums.

In the 1960s, women machinists at a Ford factory in Dagenham went on strike and lobbied Parliament, complaining that men were being paid more than them for equal work. With the backing of cabinet minister Barbara Castle, they managed to get a pay rise. Inspired by their action, women joined together to fight for equal pay for all women, and the Equal Pay Act was passed in 1970.

the Dagenham women machinists at Downing Street

But things could still be better. In the 2015 UK General Election, 1,033 women stood for Parliament; 191 were elected, the highest number ever for the UK. But that's still only 29% of MPs. The number of women in the Cabinet is still far lower than the number of men. And not all women use their right to vote. Just two-thirds voted in the 2015 General Election.

one of the 66% of women who cast their vote in the UK General Election, 2015

Note that as long as you are in the polling ation, or in a queue outside, before 10.00pm u will be entitled to apply for a ballot pa

In some countries, the situation is far worse. In Saudi Arabia, women are still seen as second-class compared to men. Whilst they have recently been given the right to vote, women there are still not allowed to drive cars, or open bank accounts without the permission of their husband, and they can't even go out in public without a man. And in Vatican City, women are still banned from voting.

So there are still a lot of improvements that could be made to women's lives. Maybe you can be the one to help make the changes in the future. It doesn't matter if you're a boy or a girl; you just have to believe in equality.

# Glossary

**activist**  a person who campaigns to bring about political or social change

**battalions**  large groups of troops who are ready for battle

**bills**  sets of proposed changes to the law to be agreed by Parliament

**cabinet**  a group of senior ministers responsible for controlling government policy

**cabinet minister**  an MP on the side of the government who is given special responsibility for a particular area, for example: education

**Chancellor**  the chief Finance Minister in the UK, who is responsible for the country's budgets

**conciliation**  an attempt to stop an argument

**enfranchisement**  given the right to vote

**folly**  foolishness

**House of Commons**  all the elected Members of Parliament

**House of Lords**  all the lords (and now ladies) who get to have a say in law-making

**martyrs**  people who are killed because of their beliefs

**Member of Parliament (MP)**  men (and now women) who are chosen by the public in the area they live to help make the country's laws

**munitions**  military weapons, stores and equipment

**opposition**  a person or group who disagrees with or has a different view on a particular topic

**Parliament**  the collective name for the elected MPs and unelected lords who run our country, but can also refer to the Palace of Westminster, which is the building in London where MPs and lords meet to debate and pass laws

**privilege**  a special right available only to a particular person or group

**puerile**  childish and silly

**rallies**  mass meetings

**Reform Act**  reform means to make changes to something; an act is a change to the law that has been agreed on by Parliament; Reform Act is the name for an act which changes laws concerning elections and voting

# Index

# Key moments in suffragette history

**1832**
Mary Smith presents the first women's suffrage petition to Parliament.

**1881**
The Isle of Man gives women the right to vote.

**1903**
Emmeline Pankhurst founds the WSPU.

**1850**

**1900**

**1866**
The Women's Suffrage Society presents a petition of 1,500 signatures to Parliament.

**1905**
The first suffrage arrests are made.

**1908**
The colours white, green and purple are adopted by the suffragettes.

**1909**
Suffragettes in prison begin hunger strikes.

**1913**
Emily Davison dies from her injuries after raising awareness for the cause at Derby Day.

**1918**
Women householders over the age of 30 are finally given the right to vote, and the right to stand for election.

## 1910

## 1920

**1910**
Black Friday

**1919**
Nancy Astor becomes the first female MP.

**1914**
War is declared and women begin to take up jobs traditionally carried out by men.

**1928**
Voting is extended to all men and women over the age of 21.

55

# Ideas for reading

Written by Clare Dowdall, PhD

*Lecturer and Primary Literacy Consultant*

**Reading objectives:**
- ask questions to improve their understanding
- summarise the main ideas drawn from more than one paragraph, identifying key details that support the main ideas
- distinguish between statements of fact and opinion
- provide reasoned justifications for their views

**Spoken language objectives:**
- consider and evaluate different viewpoints, attending to and building on the contributions of others

**Curriculum links:** History – British History beyond 1066

**Resources:** ICT for research, notebooks or whiteboards and pens

## Build a context for reading
- Ask children whether they think that men and women are equal in society and whether this has always been the case.
- Challenge children to suggest some examples of equality or inequality for men and women.
- Look at the front cover and read the title: *The Story of the Suffragettes*. Ask children to describe the image and what they can deduce from this.
- Ask children to read the blurb and then to explain what suffragettes were fighting for.

## Understand and apply reading strategies
- Ask children to read pp2–5 in pairs, identifying and extracting the key ideas in note form.
- Share their key ideas from reading and then ask children to recount how they find ideas, e.g. by skimming for key words; by scanning quickly to locate information and then reading closely to build accurate understanding.